PRAISE FOR *HOLISTIC WEALTH*

"Such a moving excerpt from Keisha Blair's book *Holistic Wealth*: 'Our education system teaches about linearity, not about what to do when this linear pattern breaks, not where to look for resilience, not the art of recovery from disruption.'" —Arianna Huffington, Founder, *Huffington Post*, Founder & CEO, Thrive Global

"This book is a page-turner. Really inspirational!" —Jen Rogers, Yahoo Finance

"This book should be required reading! Keisha Blair spells out precisely how we can achieve holistic wealth. This is sure to help YOU find purpose & have a more meaningful, happy life." —Dave Kerpen, *New York Times* Bestselling Author, *The Art of People & Chairman*, Likeable Media

"Keisha Blair's book *Holistic Wealth* is full of insight and wisdom, made all the more valuable because it's been tested and refined through her unique personal experiences." —Rhiannon Beaubien, Managing Editor, *Farnam Street* and Bestselling Author of *The Great Mental Models: General Thinking Concepts*

"An amazing story of resilience." —Amy Gallo, Contributing Editor, *Harvard Business Review* and Author of the *Harvard Business Review Guide to Dealing with Conflict*

"This book will make you more wealthy, but in ways that actually matter. If you live by the wisdom within these pages, it is almost a guarantee that your life will become better. Dive head-first into this book if you want to learn to overcome challenges in your life, live more deeply, and even get more out of your money and relationships. I loved this book, and I'm confident you will, too." —Chris Bailey, international bestselling author of *Hyperfocus* and *The Productivity Project*

"Financial wellness is often sought, but its tools are rarely taught! In *Holistic Wealth*, Keisha Blair provides interesting and important insights that can help us maximize deposits and minimize withdrawals from our holistic wealth bank accounts! —Dr. Dinorah Nieves, PhD, a.k.a. "Dr. D," coaching consultant on the Oprah Winfrey Network's *Iyanla: Fix My Life*

"Absolutely everyone needs to take the time to slow down, breathe, and re-orient themselves, but especially women dealing with trauma or change. *Holistic Wealth* will help you focus on re-building and re-emerging into the world, on your terms." —Holly Lorincz, author of the bestselling *Crown Heights*

HOLISTIC

PERSONAL WORKBOOK

WEALTH

HOLISTIC WEALTH

PERSONAL WORKBOOK

KEISHA BLAIR

Catalyst BOOKS

Mention of specific companies, organizations, or authorities, in this book, does not imply endorsement, by the author or publisher. Likewise, mention of specific companies, organizations, or authorities does not imply that they endorse this book.

Internet addresses and websites mentioned in this book were accurate at the time it went to press.

ISBN: 978-1-9991787-3-4

CONTENTS

INTRODUCTION

I created this workbook to help you figure out how to apply the lessons and strategies in my book *Holistic Wealth: 32 Life Lessons to Help You Find Purpose, Prosperity, and Happiness* to your own life. This workbook is a road map that will show you how you too can build a thriving and healthy life that prioritizes what is most important to you.

To recap the main message from my book, the traditional concept of "wealth," as defined solely by a person's net income and material possessions, needs to be revised. Women today value far more than physical assets and net earnings. They care about collecting experiences, engaging in meaningful work, and having more control over their lives. The time has come for women to become advocates for a new concept of wealth that is defined by health and well-being and a well-lived life. I hope this workbook will enable all women to find ways to embrace the concept of holistic wealth and apply it in ways big and small to their own lives.

WHAT IS HOLISTIC WEALTH?

Holistic wealth comprises several essential elements: financial savvy and independence, a life purpose and mission, spiritual connection, and generosity of spirit—all of which lead to a greater sense of wholeness and resilience in times of difficulty, as well as to greater happiness and joy on a daily basis. As you embrace these various measures of wealth, you will see that they are interdependent, each building on the others. Financial wealth without emotional and physical health has limited value. Emotional well-being is difficult to achieve without financial stability. A healthy lifestyle is the foundation for emotional resilience. By focusing on all these areas, you will build a sense of well-being that is stronger than the sum of its parts.

Cultivating holistic wealth helps us to be mentally tough and to have the *grit* to weather the inevitable storms and setbacks that life brings. We are creatures of habit, and we often operate mindlessly, making the same decisions over and over again, to our detriment, until we experience some unexpected shock to the system. This shock makes us aware that we need to be more strategic about our decisions on a daily basis. If we react to disruptions from a position of fear or just press on with our old ways, then it's almost impossible to achieve holistic wealth. By being intentional in our pursuit of holistic wealth, you can figure out where the gaps are and then focus on those weak spots. Life will inevitably throw some curveballs your way sooner or later. By planning ahead, you will equip yourself to handle those challenges with grace and strength. This will not only be a gift to you, but also to those around you who are counting on you.

HOW CAN THIS WORKBOOK HELP ME?

It's one thing to read the lessons in my book and know they're good ideas. It's quite another to do the sometimes-difficult work of integrating those lessons into your own life. This workbook is designed to serve as a bridge, enabling you to connect the ideas and lessons of *Holistic Wealth* with your own life and make them yours. You may find that you enjoy doing some of the work on your own, but you may also want to create a group to discuss your findings with. This can help you work through trouble spots, give you new ideas, and find and give support to others. Most importantly, be kind to yourself as you do this work. Some of it may come easily to you; some may be more difficult. But if you stay the course, I can assure you that you will be rewarded for your efforts.

I hope that your experience with this workbook will be both empowering and enjoyable as you learn and apply these timeless principles for achieving holistic wealth. Give yourself an opportunity to really dig into the material presented in this workbook. Here are a few tips to do so:

- Before you start this workbook and before you begin each practice exercise, go back and read the relevant sections in *Holistic Wealth*, to help you to apply it better in your everyday life.
- Share what you learn from going through these exercises with family members, colleagues and friends.
- You can use this workbook on your own, which is preferable at first for you to think deeply about the responses you've chosen, but it can also be used in a group setting or as part of a book club or small group. Perhaps starting your own **Holistic Wealth Project Group**—an accountability group—will help you to implement some of these actions in your life.

Let us begin.

Love, Keisha

PART I

CREATE YOUR INTENTIONAL LIFE PURPOSE PORTFOLIO

1

CULTIVATING A HOLISTIC WEALTH MIND-SET

A person who approaches life with a holistic wealth mind-set doesn't fear taking measured risks. They are adept at recognizing fake versus real constraints, and they have mastered the art of recovery from disruption. They don't compare themselves with others, and they face crisis with dignity and grit. They view setbacks as temporary, not permanent. Their outlook leads to a greater sense of wholeness and resilience in times of difficulty, as well as to happiness and joy in daily life.

The holistic wealth mind-set means approaching life mindfully and with the understanding that every decision and action we take represents a withdrawal from or a deposit to that holistic wealth bank account. Individuals with a holistic wealth mind-set ask themselves before making any major decision: Will this action represent a withdrawal from or a deposit to my holistic wealth bank account? Repeated withdrawals lead to bankruptcy—and I don't only mean financial bankruptcy. Similarly, some actions act like compound interest in a holistic wealth bank account. The benefits of these actions multiply over time in many different areas of your life.

Making a deposit to your Holistic Wealth Bank Account

Making a withdrawal from your Holistic Wealth Bank Account

Holistic wealth is about having an intentionally designed life. As a first step, it's important to consider where you are now. What activities constitute deposits and withdrawals in your life? Only once you take an honest look at your life today can you recalibrate these activities to achieve balance. Here are some questions to help you start this process.

1. Consider a moment in your life when you had to face a big decision. How did you go about it? Did it work out? What would you have done differently?

....

....

....

....

....

....

....

2. What is a setback that you've experienced? How did you respond to it? What have you learned from it?

....

....

....

....

....

....

3. What aspects of your life represent *deposits* to your holistic wealth bank account? Be very specific.

....

....

....

....

....

....

....

4. What aspects of your life are *withdrawals* from your holistic wealth bank account? Be very specific.

....

....

....

....

....

....

....

5. What obstacle would you like this workbook to help you overcome?

....

....

....

....

....

....

....

THE TWO MIND-SETS

I developed the table below to help you think practically about how the two mind-sets differ and learn how to recognize them.

HOLISTIC SCARCITY MIND-SET	HOLISTIC WEALTH MIND-SET
Fears taking measured risks	Doesn't fear taking measured risks
Confuses real and fake constraints	Adept at recognizing fake and real constraints
Faces crises with fear and anxiety	Faces crises with dignity and grit
Views setbacks as permanent constraints and defines people in terms of those constraints	Views setbacks as only temporary, not permanent constraints and does not define others by their current circumstances
Thinks of life in win-lose terms	Thinks of life in win-win terms
Values self above all and acts primarily in terms of ego	Values service to humanity and is not ego-driven
Does not recognize the benefits of constant spiritual self-renewal	Recognizes the benefits of constant spiritual self-renewal
Does not have a mission or a vision for themselves but is primarily drawn to outward manifestations of "success"	Has a mission and a vision in line with their core values (that is, the Law of Purpose)

HOLISTIC SCARCITY MIND-SET	HOLISTIC WEALTH MIND-SET
Has a limited view of others and their potential (primarily in terms of job title and salary and their potential)	Has an unlimited view of others and their potential
Does not fully realize the benefits of spending time in nature	Values the environment and spending time in nature
Primarily stuck in thinking that current knowledge and skills are sufficient	Is constantly learning and developing new skills in different areas
Thinks that individuals are constrained because of a lack of power	Recognizes that each of us is endowed with the power we need to achieve our purpose
Does not have a plan for the future	Plans well for the future (especially with regard to finances)
Has a limited view of financial and economic resources (thinking that the more we deploy resources, the fewer there are left)	Recognizes that both moral and economic resources are necessary for success (moral resources are skills, relationships, collaboration, and knowledge)

MINDLESSNESS AND MINDFULNESS

Figure 1 below presents a diagram that shows how a state of mindlessness in various aspects of our lives is counter to achieving holistic wealth and can lead to stunted potential.

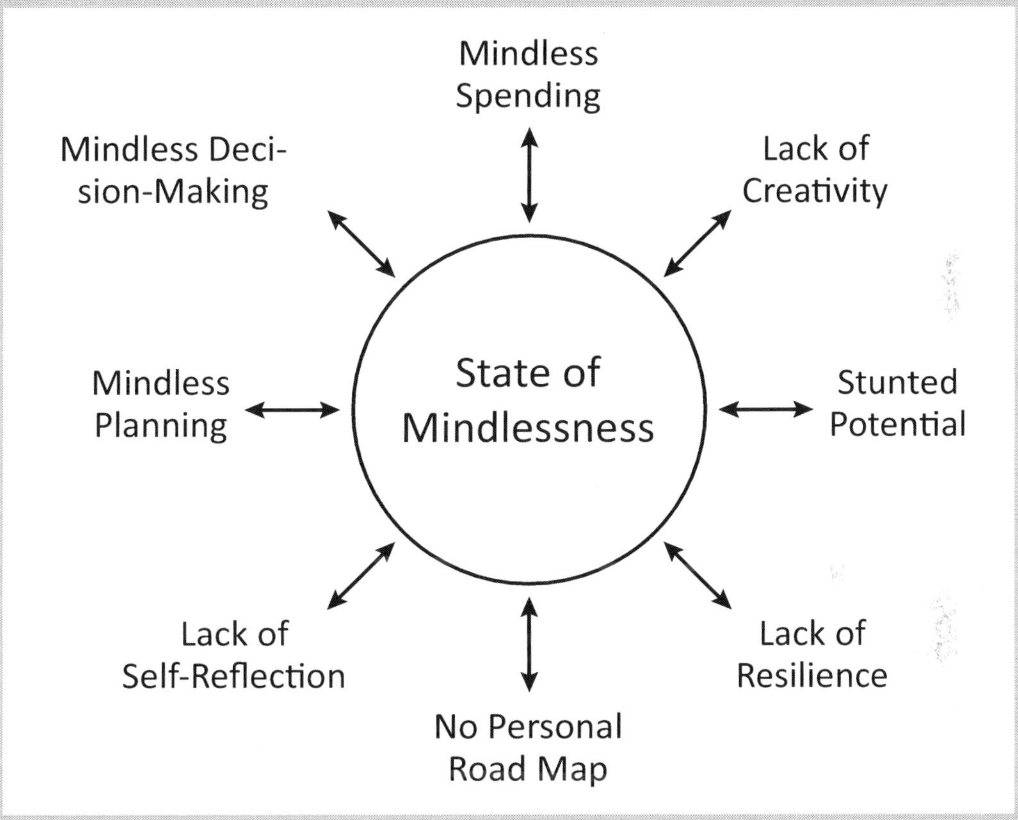

Figure 1: A State of Mindlessness Is Counter to Achieving Holistic Wealth

In contrast, Figure 2 below presents a diagram that shows how a state of mindfulness in various aspects of our lives is key to achieving holistic wealth.

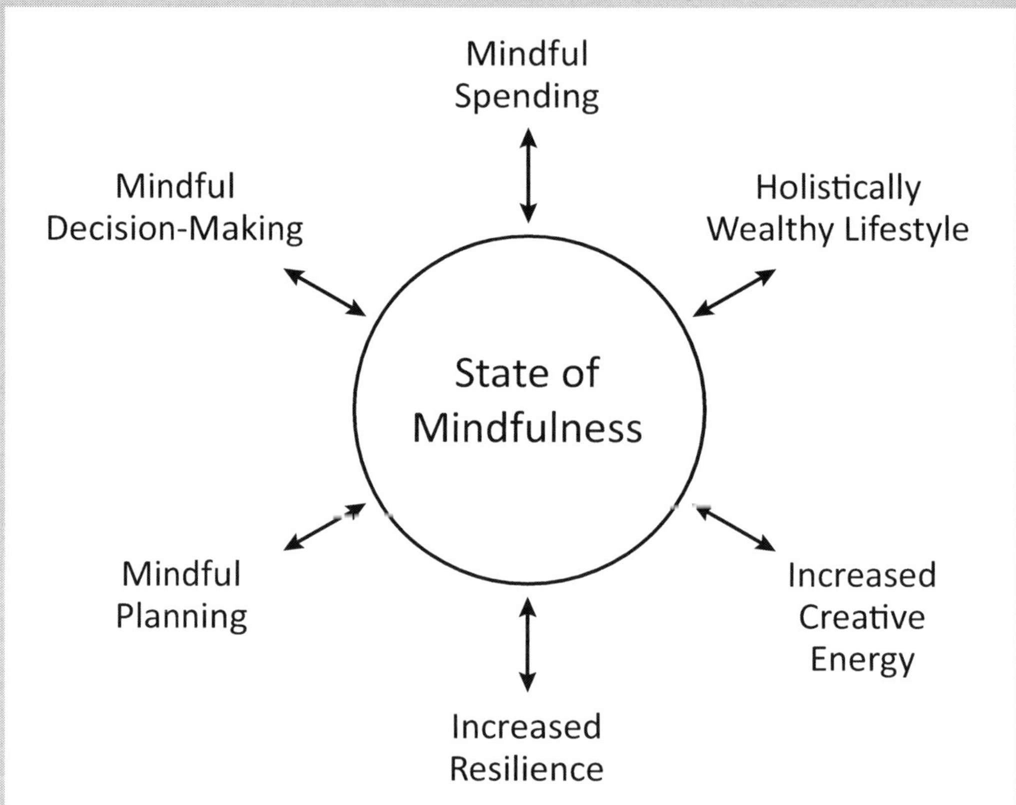

Figure 2: A State of Mindfulness Is Key to Achieving Holistic Wealth

2

THE SIX PRINCIPLES OF HOLISTIC WEALTH

The six principles of holistic wealth are timeless laws that govern every aspect of our lives. You may find that some of these principles are familiar; indeed, some are old ideas with biblical origins. However, what we are doing here is combining them in such a way that they interact and strengthen and build on each other. While there is value in each principle, there is infinitely more power in them as a whole. By embracing all of them together, I hope you will experience a real shift in mind-set that leads to great satisfaction in your daily life.

1. **The Law of Abundance** emphasizes that there are enough resources available for each of us to live an abundant and holistically wealthy life. We just need to learn to define abundance in more holistic and creative ways to fully enjoy it.

2. **The Law of Spiritual Self-Renewal** focuses on the power of prayer, mindfulness, and meditation for mental renewal. This work enables us to transition from a state of scarcity and pessimism to one of gratitude.

3. **The Law of Purpose** emphasizes that each of us has a unique purpose in life. To live a holistically wealthy life, it is necessary to seek out your own purpose and live it authentically.

4. **The Law of Reciprocity** is about give-and-take in all aspects of our lives, from finances to relationships. When we enrich others' lives, our own lives become enriched.

5. **The Law of Natural Harmony and Balance** highlights the importance of equilibrium in all aspects of life: exercise for physical renewal, spending time in nature, eating well, and nurturing relationships. Balance encourages us to attend to our priorities so that we don't neglect one area of our life in favor of another area.

6. **The Law of Continuous Learning** encourages us to keep growing. Lifelong learning is an important asset in your holistic wealth bank account and includes activities such as community endeavors and mentorship.

Consider the principles listed above and think about the ones that feel most familiar and comfortable to you—and the ones that need the most work or development. In this day and age when we are all so connected to technology, many of us struggle to achieve natural harmony and balance as well as spiritual self-renewal. The struggle extends from our professional lives to our personal lives, causing us to become burned out because of so many competing demands.

1. Which of the principles above do you feel you handle well most of the time? How do you apply them to your life? How do they make you feel?

....

....

....

....

....

....

2. Which of the principles above requires the most work and effort?

3. What are the challenges to incorporating those principles into your life?

4. Remember: achieving holistic wealth is a journey that hinges on the first steps. What three actions can you implement to integrate these principles of holistic wealth more fully into your life?

....

....

....

....

....

....

....

5. Once you have experimented with some of the actions suggested on pages 15 and 16, write down how they make you feel. Do you feel stronger and more resilient? Happier? More balanced?

....

....

....

....

....

....

....

ACTIONS THAT LEAD TO HOLISTIC WEALTH

- Start a gratitude journal.
- Attend a wellness retreat.
- Go for a walk in the woods. Use your five senses to notice nature around you.
- Invite a friend for coffee.
- Buy a pet.
- Sign up for a class.
- Go to an art opening.
- Explore a new neighborhood.
- Make a list of things you'd like to learn.
- Celebrate you with a pedicure.
- Try a meditation app.
- Turn off social media for twenty-four hours.

- Clean out your closet and donate what you no longer need.
- Spend an afternoon volunteering for a cause you believe in.
- Make a list of what's important to you.
- Bake a pie for a neighbor.
- Say no to give yourself more time to do something meaningful.
- Reread a favorite book and watch a favorite movie.
- Get in touch with an old friend.

3

DEFINING YOUR PERSONAL MISSION STATEMENT

Holistic wealth happens by design; it results from a series of strategic decisions. It is not accidental or mired in mindless activities or driven by habits. Personal mission statements are an important component of an intentionally designed life, leadership, and personal development. It forces you to think deeply about your life, clarify its purpose, and identify what is truly important to you. A personal mission statement also forces you to clarify and express, as briefly as possible, your deepest values and aspirations. It imprints your values and purposes in your mind so they become a part of you. Take time to craft your own personal mission statement and integrate it into your weekly planning as a way to keep your vision constantly in front of you.

—Holistic Wealth

It's hard to know how to get where you want to go if you don't have a destination in mind. Consider your mission statement to be a description of your destination—the objective that encourages you to prioritize what's important and set your trajectory based on your unique values and life purpose. It answers the why, the what, and the how of your lifelong goals, and it is a crucial component of an intentionally designed life.

Your personal mission statement has to be rooted in the story of you, the sum of your life experiences, and what you want to achieve in the future. It is like a blueprint for your life filled with action verbs and themes that will guide you toward a sense of abundance in every sense of the word. To begin, ask yourself these questions about your story and values.

1. Look around and name people you admire. What qualities do they have? What can you learn from their attitudes and approaches?

....

....

....

....

....

....

....

2. What is most important to you? What would you like people to say about you at the end of your life?

....

....

....

....

....

....

3. What are your past successes? These successes can be personal or professional. See if you can identify a common theme, which may help you figure out what is most important to you.

....

....

....

....

....

....

....

4. What is your unique contribution? What would you like to do most for the world? Your friends? Your family?

....

....

....

....

....

....

....

5. How would your friends describe what they admire most about you?

....

....

....

....

....

....

....

....

6. List your core values. What do you believe best identifies who you are, and what are your priorities going forward?

....

....

....

....

....

....

....

....

QUALITIES AND ASPIRATIONS

Here is a list of attributes to get you started. Which of these resonate with you?

Dependable.
Reliable.
Loyal.
Committed.
Open-minded.
Consistent.
Honest.
Efficient.

Community-oriented.
Innovative.
Creative.
Compassionate.
Adventurous.
Motivated.
Positive.

Optimistic.
Passionate.
Respectful.
Courageous.
Lifelong learner.
Persevering.

Based on your answers above, write your personal mission statement here. (Don't worry. It can evolve over time. It should feel obvious and true to you.)

....

....

....

....

....

....

IDENTIFYING AND APPLYING VALUES

The three case studies below show how to identify and apply your own values so that you can lead a life that feels aligned and good to you. Try to pick out the key motivators for the subjects of the case studies as well as their key values. Consider circling and highlighting words and phrases that resonate with you. This process will help you in crafting your own personal mission statement.

Case Study 1:

Wendy Schultz is the CEO and founder of The Simple Life Hospitality, a vacation-property management firm in Florida founded on the principles of *simple living and life enrichment through creating memories with family and friends.* Wendy recognized that her life appeared great on the outside, with a beautiful family, high-paying job, and lots of friends, but she was stressed and burned out from working long hours. She was determined to find another way. She created the following personal mission statement to guide her: *I'm on a mission to build a life I don't need a vacation from.* Her process for building her mission statement was a bit backward: "Rather than developing a statement and then living it, I began living it and then developed my mission statement." She explains how it came about: "A close friend was sick from breast cancer and passed away right before Christmas at age forty, leaving behind a husband and three kids. As I spent time with her while she battled cancer the last six years, I recognized that far too many people put off their dreams for a 'someday' in the future that may never come. I was like many others living for the weekend, getting the Sunday night stomach knots dreading Monday's arrival, and counting down the days until the next vacation, next holiday, the weekend, retirement." Wendy's friend taught her an important lesson about how to live in the NOW and inspired her to build the business she'd always wanted to start. And Wendy learned by doing: "I have challenged all the 'rules' and have found that more often than not, there is a way. Most of the things that hold us back are barriers that we create in our heads but aren't really true. I continue to knock down those barriers every single day."

Case Study 2:

As a Russian immigrant living in America, Alissa Lentz, CEO of HERO and a Forbes 30 Under 30 recipient in 2018, was bullied through childhood for not speaking English properly. She realized that being different should never be a reason to be bullied, so she started HERO to show the world that what makes you different is what makes you super. After quitting her corporate job, she traveled the world in a sales support role where she showcased aircraft at global aviation conventions. During this time, she revisited an idea that she had in college and designed, developed, and launched HERO, with this as its mission: *HERO empowers courage through accessories that take a stand for equality. Each backpack carries an empowering heroic story and provides one day of school to a girl in a developing country.* Traveling the world brought her closer to her passion for education and inspired her to launch the company as a social enterprise to support access to education around the world. Alissa never went back to the corporate job . . . instead, she launched a business founded in *a personal mission that creates a positive impact on the world.*

Case Study 3:

Vicki Mayo is the CEO and cofounder of The TouchPoint Solution and the creator of TouchPoints, a wellness device that helps kids by alleviating stress in 30 seconds. Vicki explains that after reading *The Alchemist* at age 19, she made a list of her values and things that she wanted to be known for when she died. She then created a mission statement based on that: *My greatest obligation and joy in life is to help humanity.* This mission led her to adopt two children. She then worked for her governor to change the child welfare system in Arizona and invent and commercialize the technology in TouchPoints.

4

GOALS—WITH WISDOM

When you make your goals, do so knowing that there will be detours ahead. Know that some things will be out of your control. All things are on God's own perfect timing. Put things in place and know that if a detour comes, you are a detour slayer. Achieving holistic wealth requires determination and grit. It requires an ability to pivot and change direction if need be. It requires that get-up-and-go attitude even in the face of tremendous obstacles.

—Holistic Wealth

Too many self-help books tackle the subject of goal setting by just listing ways of measuring those goals or telling people that by creating indicators of success—for example, measurable goals that are SMART (specific, measurable, achievable, realistic, and timely)—you will achieve them. I wanted to go beyond that in *Holistic Wealth*. Based on my experience, I don't believe that you will reach your objectives simply by setting SMART goals. It's about getting around detours and roadblocks and using your own instincts, strength, and wisdom to find a way to move forward. Too many goals get dropped because we face a roadblock and then can't figure out a way around it. But roadblocks don't have to mean walking away from your dreams. What I have learned is that it's all about learning to anticipate those roadblocks. You can't know everything that will be coming at you, of course, but if you know they're out there, they have less power to derail you. You just need to learn how to pause, reconsider, pivot, and find a new path. It may take you longer than you expected. You might need extra help. But the point is that you carry on no matter what. Remember this line from *Holistic Wealth*: *I am a conqueror. I am a detour slayer. And my goals and dreams don't exist in a vacuum. Every bit of my life is preparing me for something better, something greater!*

Start by determining what success means to you. If there are aspects of your life that make you feel like you are suffering from burnout, it could be that your goals and values are not well aligned. For example, you want to climb the corporate ladder, but you would much prefer to just make more time to spend with your family. Our goals are sometimes incongruent with our deepest desires, but somehow, because we feel like we have to conform to society's definition of success, we give in to these pressures and put our innermost desires on the back burner. The key here is to be really honest with yourself. It might help to have a change of scenery as you think about these bigger questions, as it can be hard to break out of your old thinking when you're in a familiar place.

1. What does long-term success look like to you? Think about your values and your personal mission statement, as well as what your ideal life would look like. What will you be most proud of when you look back on your life?

....

....

....

....

....

....

....

....

2. What are your short-term goals that will enable you to achieve that picture of success and happiness in your personal life?

....

....

....

....

....

....

....

....

3. What are your goals that will allow you to achieve the professional success you want in the future?

....

....

....

....

....

....

....

....

4. What obstacles do you foresee to achieving success? How might you overcome them? What steps will you take to get back on track when you hit a roadblock? Consider past obstacles and how you worked through those.

....

....

....

....

....

....

....

5. What are three actions that you can take today to start tackling those goals? Or consider one big goal and break it down into several microgoals.

....

....

....

....

....

....

....

SOME TIPS ABOUT SETTING GOALS

Not all goals have to be related to work. Yes, we often think of goals in terms of our professional path. But think bigger. When you look back on your life, what do you want people to remember about you? What legacy would you like to leave? Do you have health-related goals? Are there experiences you want your children to have? Is there a hobby you've always wanted to try?

Consider planning a retreat or getaway to encourage blue-sky thinking. It can be difficult to think about your big dreams when you have to buy milk, drive carpool, or work a full day. Even if it's just a hike in the woods, try to get a change of scenery.

Share your hopes and dreams! Find a friend and brainstorm together. It can be limiting to try to set goals on your own—the right friend can help you think more broadly about the possibilities. Or start a monthly discussion group (for example, a Holistic Wealth Project Group) to workshop ideas and help each other make those goals a reality.

Separate out your blue-sky thinking from planning. If you get too bogged down in how you might make it happen or whether it's realistic, you might never let yourself think big. Give yourself the freedom to dream big. You can put off figuring out how to make it happen until another day.

Celebrate your accomplishments! Sometimes we are so ambitious that we forget to celebrate the milestones when we reach them.

PART II

CREATE A LIFE OF TRAVEL AND ADVENTURE

5

SABBATICAL PLANNING

A sabbatical can ignite your passions and help you find your true purpose in life, as it allows you the free time to explore creative endeavors and helps you to identify your goals from a new vantage point. A sabbatical is a key part of helping you design the intentional life you want. It allows you to discover your unique talents and to seek your higher self through spiritual self-renewal. By disconnecting from your daily routine, you will encourage new lines of thinking and challenge yourself in new ways. Once your passions are ignited, it becomes easier to identify what makes you happy and what you want your life to look like.

I know what you're thinking. It's difficult to imagine taking that kind of time away, but I assure you that it's a goal that will pay dividends.

The first step is to identify what *your* dream sabbatical might look like. Then you can figure out how to make it happen. It's important to remember that a sabbatical doesn't have to involve a wholesale pause in your life. If you can only get away for a couple of weeks, then make that happen. The point is to disengage from the routine that absorbs most of your waking hours and consider your life from a fresh vantage point.

Here are my top tips on how to make a true and proper sabbatical a reality.

- First, map out the sabbatical you would like to take. Determine how long you can realistically break away from work and other obligations. **Consider where you would like to go.** Do some research on how much money you will need each week or month. Then pad that number.

- Second, **consider the expenses you'll still have to cover on the home front while you're away.** You'll want to continue to contribute to your various benefits while you're on sabbatical: Continue to fund any retirement accounts during this time since you won't want to delay your retirement because you took a break from work. **Consider health insurance and how you will cover yourself while you're away.** Make sure you can keep up your life insurance and long- and short-term disability insurance.

- **Consider creative ways to build your savings.** Can you rent out your home? Have a garage sale? Put yourself on a limited budget for a few months before your trip? Crowdfund it by volunteering while you're away and giving your friends a cause to support?

- **Draw up a realistic budget.** You don't want to run short while you're away, as that will prove extremely stressful. So create an Excel spreadsheet that maps out all your anticipated expenses and determine how long you can get away.

- **Get creative.** Can you stay with family or friends for part of the time? Can you volunteer in exchange for housing? Research house-sitting options or house swaps.

- **Get out ahead of it.** Obviously, the earlier you can start planning your sabbatical the better, because it will buy you more time to organize your finances and build a nice cushion.

Answers to these questions will help you begin imagining this time away and the ways it will benefit you.

1. What are some of the activities you most enjoy when not working and fulfilling your normal daily obligations?

....

....

....

....

....

....

....

....

2. Would you like to be alone or working and spending time with others?

....

....

....

....

....

....

....

....

3. Does it consist of structured time or not? Volunteering? Experiential learning? Extreme sports?

....

....

....

....

....

....

....

....

4. What is your absolute dream sabbatical? Don't hold back. If you could go anywhere or do anything, what would it look like? Remember: you can only make dreams come true if you know what they are.

....

....

....

....

....

....

....

5. How do you think time away could shift your perspective and change your life?

....

....

....

....

....

....

....

....

FAMILY SABBATICALS

I took my two children when I went on sabbatical, and we all benefited from the time away to heal and rejuvenate. I put them in schools with curriculums similar to their regular schools, while also exposing them to new experiences and immersion in a different culture. I rented my home to cover the costs of housing in our new location. I chose a place with extended family and friends to help ease the transition. And I brought all the family essentials so that the kids and I would feel more at home. I enrolled them in activities like swimming to help them make friends and learn how to adapt to a whole new world.

Road Trips

Road trips can be life altering. There's something about the open road that allows us to think and reflect, to shift into a state of mindfulness. It allows us to tap into our purpose and passions, and consider whether life is unfolding as we want it to be. Travel links us to nature, to growth, and to introspection. When we connect with new communities outside our own, it fuels resilience, self-confidence, and empathy for others. It builds an appreciation for diversity and encourages an openness that can be hard to experience in our normal routines. Road trips are so much more flexible than plane travel and encourage us to embrace the unexpected. See an attraction off the side of the road you never knew about? Feel like stopping earlier than planned? With road trips, you can change course on a whim, which can be wonderfully liberating. So if a big sabbatical isn't on the immediate horizon, consider hitting the road. Remember: the journey is the destination. You never know what you might find.

PART III

BUILD YOUR FINANCIAL INDEPENDENCE PORTFOLIO

6

LONGEVITY PLANNING

In *Holistic Wealth* I spoke about leaf-cutter ants. Leaf-cutter ants are masters of the art of productivity. They meticulously store reserves away for the future, ensuring their longevity. Looking at our savings, finances, and cash reserves like a colony that is intricate and built bit by bit is a good framework for financial resilience and planning for long-term financial security. The average person can expect to live nearly thirty years more than someone born in 1900—almost to age eighty—so it's more important than ever to plan ahead. A careful assessment of your overall health, financial status, and likely long-term care needs is essential to ensuring your well-being and financial security in the future. While it may seem far away, time and planning are your strongest allies when it comes to building a solid and secure future for yourself. You don't want to be stuck in a situation where you can't afford to retire, or you can't leave money to your loved ones. Planning ahead gives you flexibility and control.

DEVELOPING YOUR OWN PERSONAL FINANCIAL IDENTITY

A well-planned future also starts with developing your own financial identity. One way to do this is through financial literacy. Improving your financial literacy is also the greatest stimulant of wealth. Many of us make our first large purchase with a spouse or significant other. The first house, the first car, the wedding and honeymoon—these are all expenses tied to our expansionary years. We therefore transition into adulthood not having gained a full sense of our own personal financial identity. For instance, what is my investment identity? What are things I will splurge on versus save on? This can also be tied to our values and mission in life. It is highly individual. Each of us should have a financial identity—one that is distinct and separate from our spouse's or parents'. If you find yourself always wondering what your friends or parents think about the way you spend or invest, then it's an indication that you haven't fully figured out your financial identity. It's impossible to design a well-planned future without a proper financial identity—we end up living our lives in the footsteps of others, and possibly making the same money mistakes.

1. When would you like to retire, and what would you like retirement to look like? Would you like to stay in your current home or move to a smaller place? Would you like to move closer to family? Or is it important to you to remain in your current community?

....

....

....

....

....

....

....

....

....

2. How would you like to fill your days? Would you like to travel? Are there hobbies you'd like to pursue? Groups you'd like to join?

....

....

....

....

....

....

....

....

3. What expenses do you anticipate you will have during retirement? (A financial adviser can help you make sure you understand how money saved for retirement is affected by inflation.)

....

....

....

....

....

....

....

....

4. What sources of income can you expect during your retirement?

5. Do you think you may be interested in an assisted-living setting? If so, what will that cost? It might be worth looking into long-term care insurance well before you need it.

6. Have you created a will? Do your loved ones know where it is filed? Have you looked into the best ways to protect your assets for your family? An estate-planning lawyer can help ensure you have the proper documentation in place. If you have not taken care of these things, set a date to make it happen. If you're having trouble prioritizing that, consider finding a friend in the same position and making each other accountable.

....

....

....

....

....

....

....

....

ALL ABOUT DEBT

Holistic wealth is about you creating the circumstances in your life that allow you to be resilient and resourceful. This will enable you to bounce back from unexpected challenges more easily and more swiftly. To that end, paying off what you owe—whether it's student loans, your mortgage, a car loan, a credit card, or another kind of debt—is always a good thing. Being debt-free is an essential component of financial independence. It does, however, require some strategic planning and often involves some sacrifices in the short term.

There are many ways to get out of debt, and you may want help determining what to prioritize and how. You may want to channel your savings toward paying off debts in small chunks over a long period; you can look into consolidating high-interest loans so that you have a single payment to track rather than several. You may want to look into whether you qualify for a line of credit with a lower interest rate than your credit cards. You can also put automatic payment plans in place, so payments don't feel quite so onerous each month. It takes some research and hard work and sacrifice to put the steps in place, but paying off debt is like a deposit to your holistic wealth bank account. The more debt you pay off, the more unburdened you will feel.

The key to success is taking the first step and realizing that it's a long-term investment in yourself and your freedom. Most people can't get themselves out of debt overnight, but think of three or four things you can start doing right now that will save you some money right away. Once you see your savings add up, you'll feel a renewed sense of control over your financial destiny. Here are some ideas to get you started.

- Create a debt repayment worksheet and organize your finances.
- Research ways to save money on utilities: A cheaper phone plan? Lower car insurance? These won't affect your quality of life but can incrementally up your savings each month.
- Consider lifestyle changes, like eating out less or bringing your lunch to work.
- Buddy up with a friend to create accountability.
- Instead of going out to eat, start fun themed potlucks at home.
- Look into refinancing.
- Create a monthly budget and set a time to review it each week in a pleasant setting. Don't make it a chore. Challenge yourself by making a game out of seeing how much you can save.

The table below can help you organize and assess your debt. Fill it in with information on car loans, mortgages, personal loans, credit cards, investment loans, business loans, and student loans. Can any of them be consolidated? Can you find a lower interest rate? Which are your top priorities?

NAME OF LENDER	MONTHLY PAYMENT	PURPOSE OF LOAN	RENEWAL DATE	INTEREST RATE	DUE DATE FOR PAYMENT

7

TAKING MEASURED RISKS

Becoming widowed at thirty-one, eight weeks after giving birth, is a real constraint. It ain't fake. However, as I learned then, with time even real constraints can be overcome somewhat by taking measured risks. It would have been easy for me to sit back after my husband died and not take any measured risks. If I had listened to the naysayers, I would have become paralyzed with fear. I was frequently frustrated with modern self-help books after becoming widowed. They often talk as if an individual is the only variable in an equation and so is devoid of constraints. Constraints are seen as a figment of imagination. Well, some constraints are real and lasting. The good news is that you can take steps to learn how to properly identify real and fake constraints in every situation. Learning how to identify fake versus real constraints is key to achieving holistic wealth.

—Holistic Wealth

A person who approaches life with a holistic wealth mind-set doesn't fear taking measured risks. They are adept at differentiating fake and real constraints and taking measured risks, and they have mastered the art of recovery from disruption. Holistic wealth is about having an intentionally designed life—and taking risks ensures that you can make the changes that will get you the life you want. The key is to figure out how to take those risks in a strategic, thoughtful way. Too many people become paralyzed by the fear of change and therefore get no closer to living their dream life. The good news is that you can take steps to learn how to properly identify real and fake constraints in every situation. Being widowed at thirty-one, eight weeks after giving birth, was a very real constraint. However, it was also a short-term constraint, not a permanent one. Discrimination and racism in the workplace are real constraints that can lead to career stagnation and loss of income. However, thinking you can't grow your business because you have limited financial resources is a fake constraint because there are so many resources available in the forms of loans, grants, and investment. Expertise is also a fake constraint since there are always ways to learn and also to get help from mentors or outside consultants. It's important to start with how you feel about risk. These questions should provide some ways to think about it.

1. Think about a recent risk you took. How did it work out? How did you make the decision to take it? Would you do it again?

....

....

....

....

....

....

....

....

....

2. What is a risk you wish you'd taken, and where do you think you'd be now if you'd taken it?

3. What stops you from taking chances?

4. What strategies can you implement to help you think through your decisions and choices?

5. What opportunity would you like to take that feels impossible right now? Why?

HOW TO ASSESS RISKS

If you feel stuck and unsure about how to open yourself up to taking bigger chances or going after your dreams, consider some of the following steps to get unstuck.

- Gather information. Conduct research using reputable sites on the internet. Build a foundation of knowledge. Create a list of questions.
- Talk to an expert. Once you understand the pros and cons a bit better, find an adviser or consultant who can assess your situation and help you determine what level of risk to take.
- Talk to a friend. Better yet, talk to several friends.
- Talk to a mentor.
- Make a list of worst-case scenarios and think about how you'd handle those situations if they came to pass.
- Set a schedule for yourself. Don't try to tackle everything at once, or you might get overwhelmed.

PART IV

BUILD YOUR PHYSICAL, SPIRITUAL, AND EMOTIONAL ASSET PORTFOLIO

8

SPIRITUAL SELF-RENEWAL AND LETTING GO OF THE BAD

We all go through valleys and peaks, but oftentimes those valleys can seem unpassable and the mountaintop an insurmountable, faraway dream. Many of us get stuck in our valleys, while some of us can make it back to the mountaintop more agile, better than before, and ready to take on the next challenge.

What makes the difference between those who have more mountaintop moments and those who seem stuck in the valley?

Without continuous, methodical, conscious efforts to renew ourselves, we can become stuck in the "valley of dry bones." The Law of Spiritual Self-Renewal is clear here: we must examine ourselves if we are to find our purpose and live a meaningful life—a life of greatness.

—Holistic Wealth

Spiritual self-renewal is about taking time to rejuvenate, letting go of the past so a new you in a new phase of life can be born. Negative thoughts can be surprisingly powerful and toxic, intruding on our thinking and holding us back from creating the kind of life we want. By identifying them, you can begin the work of lessening their power over you and banishing them from your life. You can renew yourself and embrace a new holistic wealth mind-set.

Many of us hide metaphorical dry bones in our minds and hearts, away from full view of the world. These dry bones are thoughts that bring us down, hold us back and fuel negativity. These metaphorical dry bones are obstacles to happiness and success and prevent us from achieving holistic wealth. They might include emotions such as guilt, shame, or embarrassment, thoughts of failure, fear, anger, worry, resentment, frustration, envy, jealousy, feelings of inadequacy, and low self-esteem. The first step to renewal is to bring these into the light, look them straight in the eye, and then figure out how to slay them once and for all. The goal here is obviously to make way for the positive.

1. Start by making a list of all your "dry bones." Call each one by name—whether it's anger, fear, doubt, worry, or frustration—and then describe the triggers for these thoughts. These might be events, people, or situations that are associated with these thoughts.

2. What influence do these dry bones have on your daily life? On your hopes and dreams?

....

....

....

....

....

....

....

....

3. In what ways might these dry bones be holding you back?

....

....

....

....

....

....

....

....

4. How do they affect your interactions with friends, family members, or colleagues?

5. What steps can you take to diminish their power over you?

6. If these thoughts and feelings absorb a lot of your time, how might you move on from them or resolve them?

....

....

....

....

....

....

....

....

HARNESSING GRATITUDE AND AGENCY

One thing that can help you banish your dry bones is to focus on the positive. Scientific evidence shows that gratitude and a sense of agency are very powerful. Here are some ways you can harness those to create a positive mind-set:

- Start a gratitude journal. This can help you build a gratitude mind-set that puts your dry bones in perspective and might lessen their power over your thinking. Crowd them out with good things!
- Try meditation to be more present in the moment.
- Make a list of things that you have the power to change.
- Have a letting-go ceremony. Officially banish the negativity from your mind!
- Have a plan for what you'll do when you feel overcome by negative thoughts. Maybe you tell yourself to always go for a walk or call a friend or distract yourself in some way.
- Some dry bones might be hard to let go of. Could therapy help? Consider finding a way to address them head on. Perhaps you can then find a way to leave them behind.
- Find a way to help others.

THE MANY BENEFITS OF HOBBIES

When I was about thirteen years old, I inadvertently created a vision board of all the things I liked—and I did it on my bedroom wall. While other teenage girls pasted pictures of celebrity boy bands on their walls, I had magazine pictures of beauty products such as luscious lipstick and shiny lip gloss in vibrant colors. I also put up pictures of perfumes, with glass bottles that could be pieces of art.

To this day, interior design has remained my hobby, and when I went on sabbatical, I renovated and decorated our new space with colors that were calming and with decor items that created a cozy feel: white faux-fur rugs, white candles, white duvets, and metallics in the kitchen, with black glass cabinets and a gray and black metallic backsplash. I created my own Zen retreat. These hobbies not only got me through some rough times, but they also brought me happiness and joy. I was surrounded by beauty inside and out, and it got me through the transition period.

—Holistic Wealth

Hobbies may sound like something to do on the side, but they are what allow us to find our passions and purpose in life, and they play an important role in maintaining our state of natural harmony and balance. Joyful hobbies serve as an important creative outlet and are a big asset in your holistic wealth bank account. Hobbies are a source of satisfaction, creativity, and community, and they are a release valve for daily stresses and a time to be present in the moment. It is also good for the brain to try new things and engage in creative pursuits. Hobbies are also important because they allow us to do things we're not good at. Don't underestimate how important that is. We can explore at our own pace without the pressure of delivering results or worrying about failure. Think of hobbies as a way to tap into something joyful on a regular basis. And I know everyone feels too busy for hobbies, but it's worth seeing if you can carve out even a little time each week for something that you enjoy.

9

DAILY EXERCISE

As I mentioned in *Holistic Wealth,* a study by Princeton University researchers revealed that exercising stimulates the production of new neurons, including those that release the GABA neurotransmitter. The mood-boosting benefits of exercise occur immediately after a workout and continue in the long term.

If you aren't yet in a fitness routine, consider ways you can incorporate one. Even small steps make a difference. Several fitness influencers whom I interviewed for *Holistic Wealth,* especially moms with young kids, indicated that they exercise while doing other things, like doing squats in the kitchen while cooking dinner or doing laps up and down the stairs, because every little bit counts when time is limited. Every workout or fitness regime adds to your holistic wealth bank account.

If you're not already in a routine that works for you, it can be daunting to figure out how to fit it in. The good news is that there are now more options than ever before. Here are some questions to help you overcome the obstacles.

1. What are your fitness goals? Would you like to be exercising more? Differently?

....

....

....

....

....

....

....

2. What type of exercise brings you the most joy? Do you like working out alone or with others? Do you prefer structure or are you more self-driven? Do you prefer being outside or in a gym or studio setting? Do you enjoy routine or mixing it up?

....

....

....

....

....

....

....

3. Think of three things you can try. Perhaps it's a new exercise class or studio. Maybe it's scheduling a long hike with a friend. Or is it signing up for lessons for something totally new and different?

....

....

....

....

....

....

....

....

CREATIVE WAYS TO INCORPORATE EXERCISE INTO YOUR LIFE

- Instead of meeting friends for drinks, suggest a hike.
- Walk to work—or at least partway to work.
- Do errands on foot whenever you can.
- Buddy up. Find a friend and start a running routine with them.
- Many gyms and studios have group activities that make exercise more entertaining—glow-in-the-dark barre class, anyone?
- Take a salsa class. Or an acrobatics class.
- Try something for a month, so that it has a chance to become a habit.
- Catch up on current events podcasts while you work out.
- Get a dog that needs regular walks.
- Notice how great you feel after working out. Let that sink in.
- Think of it as a time to celebrate you, not a chore to check off your list.

PART V

BUILD YOUR RELATIONSHIP ASSET AND LEARNING PORTFOLIO

10

MENTORSHIP

Mentorship is a critical enabler of holistic wealth because it enables us to learn from others who have gone before us and creates a path to follow. Mentorship is also part of the Law of Continuous Learning and the Law of Reciprocity. Mentorship is one of the best ways we can give back to our community. It is a critical enabler that activates holistic wealth in many ways, whether you are mentoring or being mentored. Mentorship can apply to many life circumstances—whether you're looking for other new mothers or parents to connect with; other work-at-home moms; or other leaders in your community. It's important to keep in mind that mentorship doesn't only apply to professional situations.

The first step is to find the right mentor. This is not just about finding someone above you on the professional ladder. It's about making sure that they relate to and can understand the challenges you face, whether it's juggling family and work as a new mother or facing certain issues in the workplace. It's not just about building a career but building your own personal mission and aligning your entire life, including your career, around that personal mission. So if a part of your personal mission is helping women with female economic empowerment, then seeking out leaders who have similar goals will help you to further your personal mission. It's also important that you think about how you can provide value in the relationship. Be sure to ask if there are ways you can support their initiatives and efforts in the community. Always be mindful and respectful of their time. And be ready to pay it forward when the opportunity presents itself. Is there someone who would consider you an expert? See if there are ways you can support others.

1. What kind of support and advice are you seeking? Is it professional or personal? Do you need a one-on-one mentor, or is there a group situation that might help?

....

....

....

....

....

....

....

2. If you're not sure what kind of help to ask for, could a business or life coach be a good way to help you identify what sort of help you need?

....

....

....

....

....

....

....

3. Make a list of people in your industry whom you admire. Why do you admire them? If one of them can't be your personal mentor, is there another way you can learn about how that person became who they are?

4. Get creative about ways to get career advice. So many leaders give talks about how they advanced in their careers. Can you learn something from their talks? What kind of research can you do to help identify and clarify your objectives?

5. What networking groups are there in your area that could put you in touch with potential mentors?

....

....

....

....

....

....

....

....

6. What expertise do you have to offer others?

....

....

....

....

....

....

....

....

INVESTING IN MENTORSHIP

Entrepreneurs Building a Business

When Kathy Haan, CEO of Idyllic Pursuit, started her business as a health and fitness coach, she initially lost money. At her first personal development conference, she stayed with six other women in a tiny hotel room to save on expenses. She made the six-hour drive home on fumes in her gas tank. She ate one banana the entire weekend. Three years later, she was in debt up to her eyeballs, attending school full time, working full time, and the sole provider in a house of five.

She knew something had to change, and so she spent $2,000 on a mentor. A few months later, she started to turn a pretty good profit. At that point, she decided to *leave* health and fitness coaching and focus on her passion to help others launch their coaching businesses. Six months later, she started making so much that she traveled to 21 different countries within 18 months—some for business, but mostly for pleasure. People she had put on a pedestal became *peers*, then friends, then business partners. Kathy says, "I am a firm believer in *paying* for a mentor—you've got to put some skin in the game. When I invested in my first mentor, I literally did not make enough to even cover my *basic needs*. But I KNEW that things would not CHANGE if I did not get serious."

11

DEVELOPING THE RIGHT RELATIONSHIPS

True luxury isn't material, it's about people. It's the privilege of connecting with others to experience something more precious: their way of looking at things and their unique perspectives. I once read a story about Bill Clinton that explained how he sat down and filled out an index card about every person he had met that day. He recorded the specific time and place where they met, and other important personal details. He would then make a note to himself to connect with them. Over the years his collection grew to over 10,000 cards.

Suzanne Brown at Mompowerment.com and author of *The Mompowerment Guide to Work-Life Balance: Insights from Working Moms on Balancing Career and Family,* whom I interviewed for *Holistic Wealth,* has her own suggestions on developing and nurturing relationships.

- **Understand what you're looking for and why.** For example, are you looking to change jobs within your company or looking to work on a new type of project to grow a skill set? These types of differences impact who you network with, how you position yourself, and what you ask for.

- **Make the effort to create a networking plan** that includes your strategy and goals (for instance, the number of new people to meet each month and the kind of people you want to meet). Hold yourself accountable to your goals. And reward yourself in a meaningful way for hitting your goals.

- **Take time to develop relationships.** You don't want to be looking for strategic relationships when you need them. You want to develop them over time and create a natural rapport.

- **Relationships are a two-way street.** Consider what you can offer in a relationship, especially with a mentor or sponsor.

- **Prepare for each conversation.** Know what you want from each interaction so that you can guide what you cover. Consider preparing an agenda, even if you don't share it. The idea is to make the most of each chat since you'll likely not meet again for a while.

1. What are you trying to achieve with your networking?

....

....

....

....

....

....

....

....

2. What networking groups or events can you join that already exist?

....

....

....

....

....

....

....

....

3. What are some creative ways to meet people in your industry but outside of your office? Are there corporate events you can help with? Volunteer groups?

....

....

....

....

....

....

....

....

4. What skills do you have to offer others that can help you build mutually beneficial relationships?

....

....

....

....

....

....

....

....

5. What event can you create on your own? Is there a happy hour or volunteer event that you can initiate?

....

....

....

....

....

....

....

....

12

LIFELONG LEARNING

Lifelong learning is essential to achieving holistic wealth. Especially in the digital age, continuous learning is critical to our growth and success. It's important that you remain relevant and valuable in a dynamic, constantly changing environment. You want to be agile enough to change and pivot. The skills needed for the future of work are creativity, critical thinking, problem-solving, digital literacy, leadership, decision-making, communication, and emotional intelligence. The Law of Continuous Learning supports the idea that learning never ends. We need to keep pace with the changing world around us.

One tricky thing about lifelong learning is that it can be difficult to know exactly what skills you'll need in the future. A mentor, coach, or networking group can certainly help you identify what courses to pursue.

For now, ask yourself a few important questions to get yourself thinking about how to integrate new learning opportunities into your daily life.

- What skills do you perceive to be most important for advancing your career? Do you need a full degree, or can you just take a few classes?

- What is your learning style? For example, are you a visual learner? Do you do better in an informal setting or a formal setting such as a classroom?

- Are you better in a group setting or do you prefer individual learning? For instance, do you need a course in leadership training, or would it suit you better to work one-on-one with a coach? What will best help you achieve your goals in the learning setting you choose?

- When are you available for learning? Do you have free time in the evenings, or do you prefer to take time off work for short-term, high-intensity retreats or bootcamps?

- Create a timeline or calendar and map out how long it will take to achieve your objectives.

A WEALTH OF LEARNING RESOURCES

There are loads of ways to gain new skills these days. Here are a few to research:

- Short-term university courses
- Community college programs
- Vocational training
- Paid coaching
- Massive open online courses (MOOCs)
- TED Talks
- The local library

PARTING WORDS

Living an intentional life takes some dedication and hard work at first. It is my hope that you will begin to experience its rewards as you embark on this new journey. Be kind to yourself along the way. Spread goodwill. Be patient. Enjoy the moment.

ACKNOWLEDGMENTS

To the team at Girl Friday Productions, including Christina Henry de Tessan and Alexander Rigby, thank you for your support and your help in getting this workbook out into the world in excellent form.

To the various editors and publishers who gave me a platform to share my writing and experiences, such as Arianna Huffington, and the editors at *FinerMinds* (Mindvalley), who allowed me to write alongside some of the great motivational writers like T. Harv Eker and Vishen Lakhiani. To Merin Curotto, former executive editor of the *Observer*, who championed my viral article and allowed me to become a contributor, thank you. To Rob Carrick, who featured the article in the *Globe and Mail*, thank you.

To the readers on Aspire-Canada, *KeishaBlair.com*, and the *Modern Widow*—thank you.

ABOUT THE AUTHOR

Keisha Blair is a trained economist with extensive experience in the public, private, and not-for-profit sectors. She started her career working on economic development projects sponsored by the World Bank and Inter-American Development Bank. She was a senior economist working in economic development and corporate finance, which included working on several federal budgets. She was part of the prime minister's supporting delegation to the World Economic Forum in 2018 as well as the East-Asia (ASEAN) Summit in Singapore. Her viral article, "My Husband Died at 34; Here Are 40 Life Lessons I've learned From It," originally published on *Thrive Global*'s website, was featured on or linked to by over 160 websites and viewed by over fifty million people worldwide. She is a graduate of the Executive Leadership Program at Harvard University's John F. Kennedy School of Government. She is the founder of several nonprofit initiatives, including Aspire-Canada (as well as the Aspire-Canada memorial scholarship). She has been featured in the *New York Times*, the *Harvard Business Review*, *Essence* magazine, the *Wall Street Journal*, the *Observer*, and many other publications. Keisha has a master of science in public policy from Carleton University in Ottawa. She lives with her family in Ottawa, Canada.

CONNECT WITH KEISHA BLAIR (USE THE HASHTAG #HOLISTICWEALTH)

I absolutely love connecting with my readers. Join the Movement for Holistic Wealth on my website www.holisticwealthbook.com. Sign the petition on the website to add your voice to the movement to ensure that every man, woman, boy, and girl around the globe can achieve holistic wealth in their lifetime.

Here's how you can connect with me:

1. Sign up for the newsletter and email me on www.KeishaBlair.com

2. Share your own stories of Holistic Wealth (#HolisticWealth and #HolisticWealthbook) and connect with me on Twitter: @KeishaOBlair

3. Follow me on Facebook: https://www.facebook.com/keishablairauthor/

4. To provide feedback or ideas on the book or the movement on holistic wealth, you can email me at info@keishablair.com

5. Follow me on Instagram: https://www.instagram.com/keishaoblair/

Book clubs: Please download the reading guide at www.keishablair.com to guide your book club discussions. You can also share recipes from the website with your book club meetings to enjoy!

Made in United States
Troutdale, OR
04/02/2024

18890974R00058